Allergies

BY MICHELLE LEVINE

amicus
high interest

Amicus High Interest is an imprint of Amicus
P.O. Box 1329, Mankato, MN 56002
www.amicuspublishing.us

Library of Congress Cataloging-in-Publication Data
Levine, Michelle, author.
Allergies / by Michelle Levine.
    pages cm. — (Living with—)
Summary: "Describes what it is like to live with allergies,
what their symptoms are, and how they are treated"— Provided
by publisher.
Audience: K to grade 3.
Includes bibliographical references and index.
ISBN 978-1-60753-477-8 (library binding) —
ISBN 978-1-60753-690-1 (ebook)
1. Allergy—Juvenile literature. 2. Allergy—Treatment—Juvenile
literature. I. Title. II. Title: Allergies.
RC584.L485 2015
616.97—dc23
                                        2013032336

Editors: Kristina Ericksen and Rebecca Glaser
Series Designer: Kathleen Petelinsek
Book Designer: Heather Dreisbach
Photo Researcher: Kurtis Kinneman

Photo Credits:
Mauritius/SuperStock, cover; Mike Booth/Alamy, 5; Tetra
Images/Alamy, 6; Blend Images/Alamy, 9; Science Picture Co/
Science Faction/SuperStock, 10; BOULAY/BSIP/SuperStock,
13; Exactostock/SuperStock, 15; Tim Gainey/Alamy, 17; Qrt/
Alamy, 18; BSIP SA/Alamy, 21; CARDOSO/BSIP/SuperStock,
22; Science Photo Library/Alamy, 25; David Young-Wolff/
Alamy, 26; ktaylorg/iStock, 29

Printed in the United States of America at Corporate Graphics
in North Mankato, Minnesota.

10 9 8 7 6 5 4 3

Table of Contents

What Are Allergies?

It's time for lunch. You are hungry! You take a bite of your sandwich. It tastes funny. Is that peanut butter? Your mouth tingles. So does your throat. Oh, no! Now your stomach hurts. What is happening? You may have an **allergy**.

Many schools no longer serve peanut butter due to allergies.

5

Bee stings hurt. They are even worse if you have an allergy.

People with an allergy have a **reaction** to common things. Foods such as peanuts can cause a reaction. Pets, bee stings, and dust can too. Some people are allergic to types of medicine or soap. All of these things have **allergens**.

An allergen can cause many **symptoms**. You may get a runny nose or a rash. You may vomit or get a stomachache. You may find it hard to breathe. Most of these symptoms are not dangerous. You get better soon. You just have to stay away from the allergen.

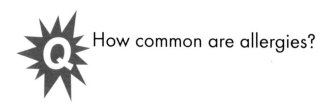 How common are allergies?

Sneezing is a common allergic reaction to dust.

 In the United States, about 50 million have allergies. That is one in five people.

This virus has been made large so you can see it. Germs are tiny. But they can make you very sick.

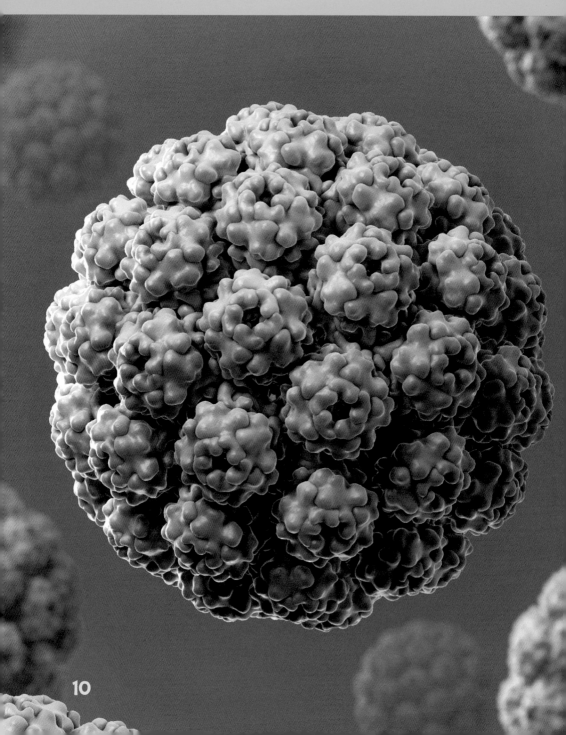

What Causes Allergies?

Some people's bodies treat allergens like **germs**. Germs make you sick. They give you a cold or fever. But your body is smart. It knows how to fight germs.

Your body makes **antibodies** to fight germs. Then the body gets rid of the germs. And you stay healthy.

An allergen is different. It does not harm you unless you are allergic to it. If you are, your body will think it is harmful. Your body attacks it like a germ. Your body makes antibodies. But this does not help. It makes a person feel sick.

Are you sick? An allergy can feel a lot like a cold.

12

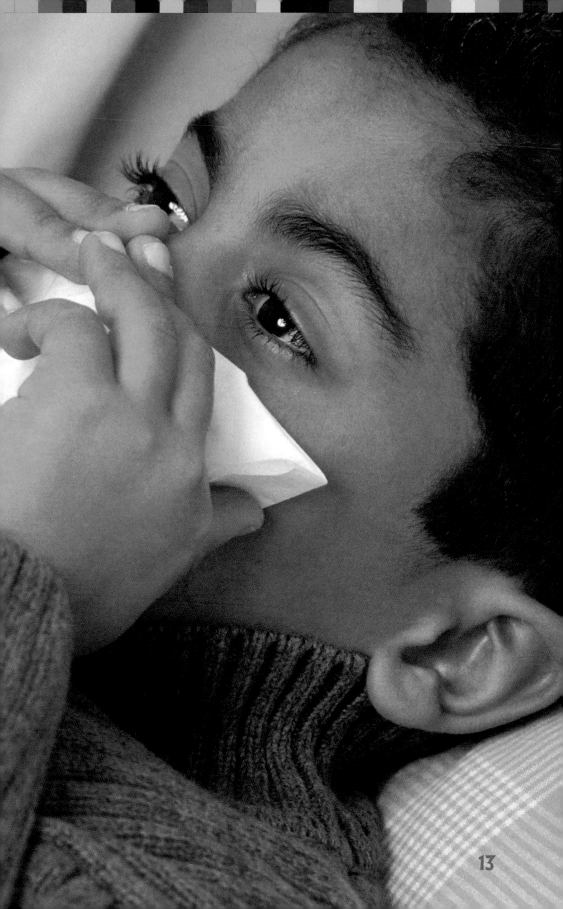

Tree nuts are healthy. But if you have a nut allergy, they can make you sick.

 What foods are people allergic to?

Types of Allergies

There are many types of allergies. Food allergies are one kind. Some people can't eat certain foods, like strawberries or nuts. They will get sick. They may get a rash or runny nose. Their stomach may hurt. Their mouth may swell. It may be hard to breathe.

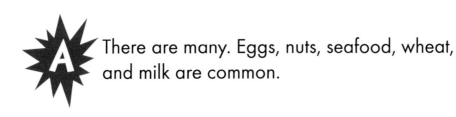
There are many. Eggs, nuts, seafood, wheat, and milk are common.

Ah-choo! Many allergies affect your nose.
Pet fur and dust may make you sneeze.
Pollen from flowers, grass, and trees
can make you sneeze too.

We all breathe these in. But they
make people with allergies get a stuffy
nose or itchy eyes. Some people have
trouble breathing.

 What is a pollen allergy called?

Pollen floats in the air. It can land in our eyes and noses.

A Hay fever is one name for it.

A bug bite can make a person's skin swell.

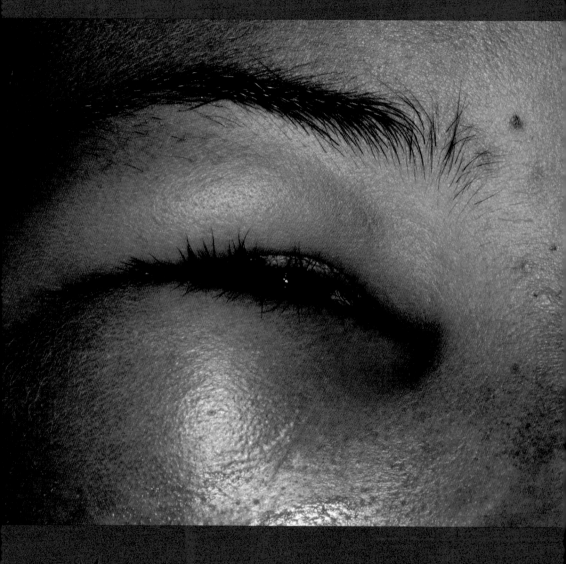

Q Can you catch an allergy like a cold?

Ouch! A bug bite! Some allergies cause a reaction on the skin. Bites and stings may cause a skin reaction. So can soap, metal, and lotion. Latex, a kind of rubber in balloons and rubber gloves, is a common allergen. It may make the skin swell. It may cause a rash. Some people even throw up. Or they can't breathe well.

 No. Allergies do not spread. Many run in families. They are passed down from parents.

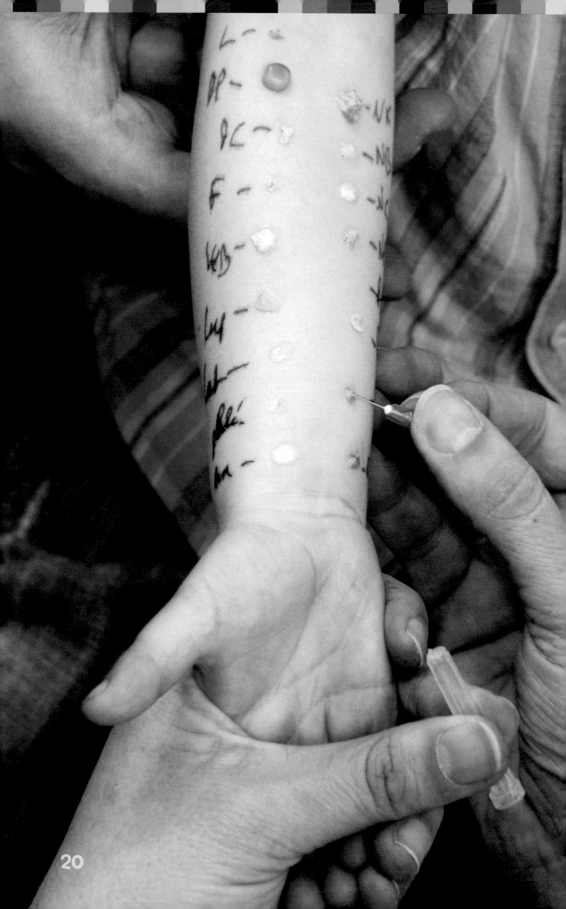

Treating Allergies

Allergies have no cure. But medicine can help. At the clinic, a doctor does a test. She puts an allergen on a person's skin. Then she pokes it. If it swells, there is an allergy. The doctor might test the person's blood too.

Doctors keep track of the allergens they test.

Most allergies are not dangerous. You may feel icky. Or you may get a rash. But those problems will go away. You just need to stay away from the allergen.

Allergy pills can make people feel better. Creams can help rashes. Eye drops help itchy eyes. Nose drops help stuffy noses.

 Does a rash mean you have an allergy?

Medicine can help some allergy symptoms go away.

 Not for sure. Other things, such as an infection, can cause a rash. It is hard to tell the difference.

Some people carry an allergy shot. They are ready in case their symptoms happen too fast.

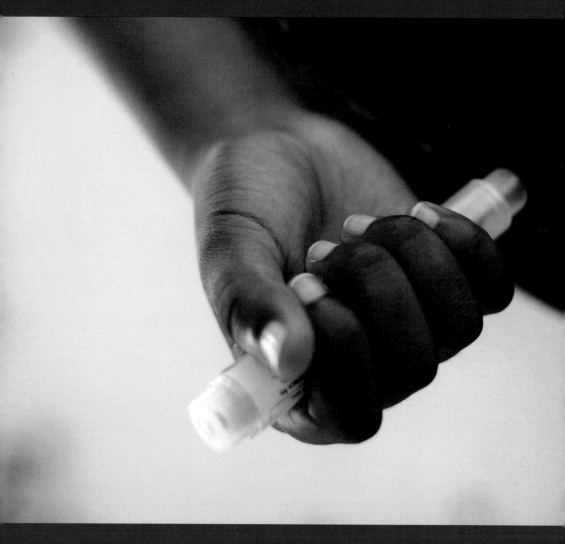

Q If you have a severe allergy, what else should you do?

A severe allergy makes people very sick.

It is dangerous. It can even lead to death.

People with a severe allergy carry medicine.

It comes in a shot. They take it when they

are exposed to an allergen. It works fast.

But they still need to go to a hospital.

 Wear a **medical alert** bracelet. It tells others about your allergy in case you can't talk.

Living with Allergies

How do people with allergies stay healthy? They keep away from allergens. Some people have a pet allergy. They don't have furry pets. Some have a dust allergy. They keep their homes clean. Some have a food allergy. They read food labels. They look for allergens in the ingredients. They don't eat foods that have an allergen.

 How long does an allergy last?

People with a food allergy must be careful of what they eat.

A Many allergies last for a person's whole life. But some people outgrow them.

Families can find recipes that everyone can eat safely.

28

How can you help? Be careful with food. If your friend has a food allergy, check with his parents before you share a snack.

Play inside with friends who are allergic to pollen. Keep pets away from people who are allergic to them. And clean up your home. It helps people with a dust allergy. Then everyone can feel good!

Glossary

allergen Something that makes a person with an allergy feel sick.

allergy A reaction caused by something that is harmless for most people.

antibody A substance in the body that fights sicknesses.

germ A tiny living thing that causes illness inside the body.

medical alert Information about a serious allergy or other illness. Medical alerts help doctors know how to treat a person who is sick.

pollen A fine, powdery dust made by flowers and trees.

reaction The body's response when it comes into contact with an allergen.

symptom Something that shows you have an illness or allergy, such as a rash or a runny nose.

Read More

Ballard, Carol. *Explaining Food Allergies.* Mankato, Minn.: Smart Apple Media, 2010.

Pistiner, Michael. *Everyday Cool With Food Allergies: Conversation Starters For Kids & Caregivers.* Newton, Mass.: Parent Perks, 2010.

Robbins, Lynette. *How to Deal With Allergies.* New York: PowerKids Press, 2010.

Simons, Rae. *What Causes Allergies?* Vestal, NY: Village Earth Press, 2012.

Websites

Kids Health—Food Allergies
http://kidshealth.org/kid/ill_injure/sick/food_allergies.html

Just for Kids: Allergies and Asthma Games, Puzzles, and More—AAAI
www.aaaai.org/conditions-and-treatments/just-for-kids.aspx

Index

About the Author

Michelle Levine has written and edited many nonfiction books for children. She loves learning about new things—like allergies—and sharing what she's learned with her readers. She lives in St. Paul, Minnesota.